Tears of ABUSE

Debra Lyn Carlton

NEWMAN SPRINGS PUBLISHING
320 Broad Street
Red Bank, NJ 07701

First originally published by Newman
Springs Publishing 2024

ISBN 979-8-89308-669-0 (Paperback)
ISBN 979-8-89308-670-6 (Digital)

Printed in the United States of America

Chapter 1

IN THE BEGINNING

I don't remember much of my childhood before the age of nine years. My friends had lots of memories; I had a lot of confusion. They say sometimes that, when you have a traumatic event in your life, your brain tries to protect you by blocking your memory. Physical and emotional abuse can be extremely traumatic; for me, it was a normal childhood.

I was born and grew up in Grand Haven, Michigan, until I was nine years old. Now I remember bits and pieces, like a kitten crawling up the living room drapes, a small black-and-white TV set on a metal cart with wheels, and a nice man who would bring me a gift once in a while. I remember we had a dog, a Doberman pinscher; his name was Mickey.

During the night, as I peacefully slept, all of a sudden I awoke in so much pain, just screaming! Mickey had my leg in his mouth, blood all over my pajamas and his face. My mom pulled him off of me; she said that he just thought he was eating a big bone. I can't remember anything else about that. However, I did have a brother named Scott, who was four years younger than I was. Sometimes I would hear munching coming from my closet, where the dog food was kept. Oh yes, it was Scott eating the dog food. He would also take the milk bones away from the dog and eat them. Yep, that was my closet, the one that would plague me in my dreams.

All of a sudden, at age fifty-four, I started dreaming of this evil woman who would lock me in that closet. Being so young, I was just horrified of the dark. As I screamed, "Mommy, mommy, please let me out, I promise to be a good girl," I was just waiting for those awful monsters to get me in the dark.

One morning, Scott was eating Trix cereal when I made him laugh; well, cereal and milk came streaming out of his nose, bouncing off the table onto the floor! It was the funniest thing I had ever seen! I got a slap across the head for that one from mom. That doesn't even measure up to when Scott and I were jumping on my bed. As I pushed him off, he hit the dead-bolt and knocked out his four front teeth. Poor kid, I really did feel bad about that one.

My mom's name was Tammy, and my dad's name was Walt. Little did I know that he was my stepdad. I was always told he was my dad, my real dad. I wouldn't know about this secret until I was fifteen years old. In the meantime, he and mom abused Scott and me terribly throughout the years. They dragged us around from city to city and state to state, running from the law the whole time.

As many siblings fight, my brother and I were no exception. We would discretely spy on each other, just waiting for that one little slipup that would make us the hero. The other, oh well, you know what happens to the other.

One day, "the nice man" took Scott and me to the Coast Guard Festival Carnival. See, every year, there is a great carnival, parade, and fireworks show. Grand Haven, Michigan, is Coast Guard City USA; it is located right on Lake Michigan, and it is a very big deal! When we were done with our fun for the day, running back to the car, I yelled, "Jim, unlock my door first."

Jim replied, "Don't call me Jim, just call me dad."

Well, Scott said, "Can I call you dad too?"

Jim laughed. "Of course you can!" He dropped us off at home. I could not understand why he said to just call him dad, so I asked mom, and she said not to listen to him because he was sick in the head. My little mind could not comprehend why mom would let a man who was sick in the head take us to a carnival. I didn't have long to think about it since my mother told us that we would be going on an adventure, moving out of state. Born and raised in Michigan, I've known no other place to call home. I was not a happy camper; we were packed up and out of there by the end of the week. We moved to Missouri and moved in with a family that I've never met before, but apparently mom and dad knew them.

Behind their house was a fireworks factory. Walt would be making the fuses for them, then I would learn how to put the fuses in the fireworks. After five years went by, we heard on the news that many people had been killed in a fireworks factory explosion in Missouri. Yes, it was theirs. It was so sad to hear that news.

Moving meant going to a new school, and that was horrifying for me. That fear started me sleepwalking. My mom would pull me out of the bathtub as I was urinating in it. She would also ask me where I was going at night; I'd tell her I was going to the bathroom. Then I would walk into closets, and she would pull me out again and again. I even got up one night, emptied a whole box of cereal on the floor, and then poured a full gallon of milk over it.

My mother remarried when I was two years old; Walt had some money, and she did like money. I wonder if she even thought about me; I doubt it. About six years before she married him, he was out with friends. They tracked down their prey, then they attacked her—a helpless fifteen-year-old, mentally challenged girl—and gang-raped her. He and all of his hoodlums were caught, and all did jail time. Not enough, in my opinion, but they were all under eighteen, so they couldn't be tried as adults. Now my mother knew this; she had a two-year-old daughter. How could she do that to me? Who does that to a child?

I only found this out because I told my aunt Sharon I wanted to be hypnotized because I couldn't remember anything before nine years old. She made me swear never to have that done, and then she would tell me a secret. She was so adamant about it that I swore to it, and then the secret was told. I confirmed this with other family members. Feeling hurt and very angry, I wanted to have the hypnosis done, but I couldn't break my promise. She said there's a reason I can't remember, and it's best to let sleeping dogs lie. If you discover something unpleasant, you just can't forget it now, because now you know it.

Chapter 2

MEAN MOMMY

As my grandma and aunt Sharon knocked on the apartment door, the fed-up landlady opened our door with her keys. "I am so tired of hearing that poor baby cry all day and night." They walked in and calmed me down, then Grandma went to the refrigerator to put some milk in a bottle for me. All that was in there was a quart of spoiled, stinky milk. Grandma was so angry with mom; now she knew that I was not being properly taken care of. See, mom worked two jobs; she came home in between jobs. Oh, mommy dearest was home. As soon as that door opened, Grandma put her over her knee and whooped her ass. Then Grandma took me home, and off to a foster home I went for one year.

After a year, I was back home with mom. Now you would tend to think she'd straighten up! But one day, on a surprise CPS visit, the social worker asked mom why I had cigarette burns all up and down both arms. Her response was that I kept on grabbing them out of the ashtray and burning myself with them. She didn't believe her, so off I went into foster care again for the next two years. I always wondered where I got all these small round scars from or even why I had them. What kind of mother does that to her little girl? A very cruel, evil woman, and it kept on coming! I had no idea this happened until I kept having dreams of a winding driveway, a dark house, crying in a drab basement, not understanding where I was or who the strangers all around me were. When my grandma explained this to me—that this was my foster home both times and why I went there—I wondered why, after twenty-four years, I would dream of this over and over again for two months. My grandma died the very next month. I was very grateful to have that information that she gave me. I have never taken death well, and this funeral was extremely hard for me. Relatives were coming up to me, touching my stomach, and telling me how she couldn't wait for this baby to be born. The first grandchild on both sides of the family, the first great-grandchild for her. After a couple of weeks, Amber Lyn, our first beautiful daughter, was born. Our sweet little baby, so perfect in so many ways. I just wish Grandma could have seen her.

I also was informed that my real father came to pick me up on his visitation day. Poor Walt didn't like it, so he took his gun out and pointed it at Jim and me. "Put her down, or I will shoot to kill you!" yelled Walt.

So Jim, my real/biological father, put me down and left. Brokenhearted at yet another failed attempt to get his little girl on his visitation time, the court had fixed everything up so my dad would get his time with me. Tammy was an evil woman; she was screwing around with Walt while my father was working his ass off in the Air Force. At other times, he would come to pick me up, and I would not be home. My conniving little mother always knew when his visitation days were, and she made it a point not to be home. She and Walt were so cruel to him. When you use your children as leverage tools, everyone suffers—except the mean ones!

At nine years old and going into the fifth grade, it was very difficult. On the first day, I asked to be excused to use the bathroom. When I hadn't returned for a while, the teacher came in, found me hiding out in the stall crying. She tried to comfort me, which I was quite amazed by; I thought I would be punished. She calmly said I could come back to class when I felt like I could. It took awhile, but soon I started to fit in.

Summer was here, and we were thrilled. That meant summer vacation. My mom and Walt would not give me a choice; I had to work in the fireworks factory putting fuses into M-80s that they illegally made. I was promised a wage, so at the end of summer, I asked for my money. Walt told me the roof over my head and food in my stomach was my pay. "Get the hell out of my way, and don't ask again."

So upset and angry, I did the only thing I could do. I buried my head in the pillow and quietly cried myself to sleep. We moved from Stanton, Missouri, to Bourbon, Missouri, into a single-wide mobile home. My parents always fought, but this one particular evening, my mom hit the floor. My brother and I were so scared.

She couldn't breathe. I grabbed Scott's hand and ran to the neighbors. With tears streaming down our faces, we banged on the door. As luck would have it, she was home, and she was a nurse. Running to our home, she placed a paper bag over mom's mouth, and she returned to her regular breathing. The nurse asked my mom what had happened. My mom's reply was, "Oh, I tripped over the rug and fell."

Liar! Liar! Walt had pushed her. Why would she stick up for him? I just could not understand it; why would she allow him to treat her like that? As three months passed, we moved to another trailer, and it had three bedrooms. Yeah, I didn't have to share a room any longer! My room was so small, I had a single bed, and there were drawers in the wall. I could barely walk sideways to get out of my room. But that was okay because I didn't have to share with my annoying little brother anymore! I was turning ten years old. Mom had asked me what I wanted for my birthday. My reply was a horse; that's all I ever wanted—nothing else. Well, of course, I didn't get one. Oh well, maybe next year, I would always tell myself.

Chapter 3

CRUEL INTENTION

Kids in school would not stop talking about what their dad did for a living; I never paid too much attention to this. Until one day, I really started to ponder over this silly job deal. Asking my mom about this, her reply was that he worked in a factory. I believed her; I shouldn't have, but that's what kids do—they believe their parents.

One hot summer day, a baby bunny was hopping in our burned-up grass. I gently picked her up and brought her in to show mom. She said since I picked it up, the mother would kill it now. "How stupid could you be?" she barked at me.

I begged to keep and bottle-feed it.

She bellowed, "Maybe this will teach you a lesson!" That night, I heard the baby bunny crying for her mother over and over again, then all of a sudden, terrible squeals! I knew the baby bunny had been killed; it was all my fault. I learned that night that I was a terrible person. Mom had always told me that; now I realized she was right. That night, my heart was heavy, and my pillow was soaked with tears as I cried myself to sleep.

As the days went by, we unhappily went back to school. Summer vacation was over, and I was yet in another new school.

There was a boy on the bus named Chris. He asked if he could sit with me. I liked him, so I told him yes. Every day, he would get on the bus and sit by me. We became friends. Then he asked if he could be my boyfriend. Well, I told him okay. We would hold hands on the bus to school. When we reached the school, we would go our separate ways until we got on the bus to go home again. I had the most beautiful long hair. It was past my butt, and when I sat down, I would sit on it. One day, I came home from school and decided to tell mom that I had a boyfriend. Bad idea. She freaked out! I told her we only saw each other on the bus and only sat by each other.

Psychotically screaming at me, she yelled, "How would Chris like you if I cut all of your long hair off?"

"No, mommy, please, I will do anything, please don't cut my hair!" I had no choice; I had to run away. I told her this, and then she told me she would help me pack. Well, off I went on my bike to my friend's house. My friend hid my bike and suitcase, then brought me into her parents' house. I stayed a few hours and decided I better get home and face the music.

The first thing mom said was that she was going to whip my ass. I figured as much. She grabbed her bamboo stick and beat me. Then Walt came in and beat me with his leather belt, which had a very thick Colt 45 belt buckle on it. The next day, I was sore with bruises, welts, and blood blisters, but that wouldn't be the end of it. Mom made me sit in a chair and told me not to move; she was going to cut my hair. I watched my long, beautiful hair dropping to the floor. One more desperate plea, begging for my hair, I cried. That was it. I should not have talked because I just made her more angry, and then she blew it. She doubled up her fist and punched me right in the eye. "I told you not to move or make a sound, so that was your own damn fault!" Who punches their ten-year-old child in the eye?

Well, needless to say, on Monday, I had to go back to school with my hair cut up to my ears and a black-and-blue eye. My boyfriend broke up with me, and no one wanted to sit by or even talk to me. I was the ugly little toad in school, and my mother was thrilled!

Finally, after a few days, a little red-haired girl named Patti asked me what happened. That's when I learned how to make up excuses, like I fell off my bike, or the most used was I fell down the stairs. A few months later, we moved again to another city, Stockton, Missouri. We moved to a house in the country. My brother and I enjoyed the woods and climbing trees. Unfortunately, this would not last long. Two months after moving into our nice country home, mom met us at the bus stop. We jumped into the car, wondering what was wrong.

"Your father has left us!"

"Why and where did he go?" I asked, trying not to show how happy this made me.

"He has gone back to Michigan to meet up with that whore Rita."

OMG! Rita was mom's best friend. Dad called that night. We were in bed, Scott came running into my room. "Deb, can you hear mom crying and yelling on the phone?" Just then, mom came into the room and said, "Your father wants to talk to you. I want you to tell him that you miss him and want him to come back home." Scott did not have a hard time doing this. I saw my mother crying and felt sad for her, so I did it too.

The next day, we came home from school, and the car was gone. Walking into the living room, the white carpet had black hair all over it. Well, Walt was back and brought Rita with him. Oh yeah, she had black hair.

I don't know why he brought Rita back, but mom got a hold of her, hence the hair on the carpet. She ended up flying back to Michigan after a few days. Her poor husband took her back only to find out that she was pregnant with Walt's son. They decided to raise the boy as their own. Mom and dad were back together again. I was hoping that things would be better, but I was wrong again. They decided to uproot us and move to California this time.

Grass Valley was beautiful; that's where mom and dad's friends lived. As we drove up the steep mountain, it seemed like it took forever—the winding road with no guardrails. We were also going to have to be on alert for the mountain lions, rattlesnakes, and cottonmouth snakes. Claude was married and had three daughters. Walt would be making M-80s for him. Later, Claude would regret this decision because Walt and mom turned state evidence against him. We spent the night there, then it was time to go to Auburn. That was the city we were going to live in—another school to go to, but it wasn't too far from Grass Valley. I always came along to visit our friends in Grass Valley; however, this time I had to stay home because of so much homework. It was dark, and strange that they were not home yet. They did not like to drive on the mountain at night. With no guardrails and very steep drops, it was very dangerous. The phone rang. Mom said our little silk terrier, Mousey, had been torn up by a mountain lion. He was still alive but shredded beyond repair, so he was put to sleep. It was all my fault. If I had been there, I would have watched him, like I always did. Oh, and mom told me if I had done my school-work in school, Mousey would still be alive! But I could not help it; I had work assigned to me. But I did feel guilty—guilty because I always kept him right by my side, and she was right.

Settling into our new apartment, I was ten years old and didn't want to share a room with my rotten little brother. That was the wrong thing to say to my mother. Out came the bamboo stick, and on went the beating. That hurt so bad, and the marks that were left were awful. Long welts on my arms, back, and legs—bruised, welted up with blood blisters on top. It gets very hot in California, and I had to learn how to wear blue jeans with long-sleeve shirts so nobody would ask what happened to me. Mom and dad would always take their vicious anger out on my brother and me. When Scott was getting beaten, I would feel so bad for him, but there was nothing that I could do. Big sisters are supposed to take care of their younger siblings. I couldn't do it now, but someday I would protect both of us.

One hot summer day, my friend Marci was moving. I asked if I could help. "Well, of course," her mom and dad both replied in synchronicity. I then asked why they were moving in the daytime because we had always moved at night. Her parents laughed. I thought it was odd that they never answered me. Of course, now I realize that they were always skipping out on their rent and, oh yeah, also running from the Feds.

That's right, my dad Walt was making illegal fireworks, M-80s, again. The Feds were watching us from their cars; also, the phone lines were popping, which means they were tapped. Well, two years in Auburn was staying long enough in one spot, so we had to move to Sacramento. Off to another school and trying to fit in again—that's just something you never really get used to.

Chapter 4

TEARS AND FEARS

My brother and I really loved to fish, and I had just bought a pocket fisherman, so after school, we went to try it out. I could feel my skin burning in the hot California sun; I couldn't take it any longer! The golf course was right behind us, with this huge shady pine tree calling my name. I told Scott we would run under it and not let anybody see us. We made it, and the coolness was just heavenly.

Then I came up with a fantastic idea! When the golf balls came by the tree, we should run out and snatch them up before the people came. Later, we could sell them. So at the end of the day, we would take all the golf balls, wash them, and then sell them for a quarter a piece, which was pretty good in the 1970s. We really cleaned up for a whole week, until one day I was selling one to a guy and it had his initials on it. Wow, could he run! Needless to say, we didn't do that again!

Opening the door to the house, I turned to give my brother that look like, "Watch out, mom and dad are fighting again." Yelling and swearing at each other, I hated it. Mom was totally pissed, and I knew to stay out of her way. The next day, coming home from school, I went straight to my room, did my homework, and then went to the kitchen to get a glass of refreshing milk. I was always on the honor roll, pulling A's and B's; it was difficult, but I had been warned of severe punishment if I didn't obey and stay on the honor roll. Mom asked me if I had done my homework, and I replied, "Yes, it was all finished."

"You lying little bitch." Then the hitting started, along with the punching. I cowered on my bed, sobbing, with my face full of tears. At thirteen years old, I was getting so sick of this! I was hurt physically and mentally, and I was angry. I wanted to run out into the street and yell as loud as I could, "*My mom and dad beat my brother and me. Can anybody help us?*" But I knew there was no help; this would only lead to more beatings, so it was best not to say anything at all. Who would believe a child over an adult anyway?

The Feds were hot on their heels again, so we went to Philadelphia, Pennsylvania, where Walt had a friend who wanted him to make many M-80s for him. We stayed in a hotel for two months; by that time, we started looking for an apartment. By the end of the day, walking into the hotel room, we turned the news on, and surprise, there was Walt's friend being arrested for Mafia activities and many other crimes, so off we went again. I was happy to be back in Michigan, but so much had already changed.

Another school, but this time I knew one person, a little girl I had known since second grade. We remained friends and pen pals throughout the years; now it was going to be great to go to school again with Kathi. She introduced me to a lot of people and to a couple of cheerleaders, Jill and Kristi. Kathi was a rally girl; they were all loud, jumping around, and not shy at all. Me, I would rather hide in a corner and not say a thing. Kristi always had a boyfriend, so Kathi, Jill, and I would always hang around together, and pretty soon, Jill and I became best friends also. Jill really hated my parents because she soon realized how abusive they were to me. The abuse never stopped for us, mentally or physically. Walt's weapons of choice were his thick Colt 45 belt buckle with his leather belt; mom's was her bamboo stick. Both of which left wicked welts, bruises, blood blisters, and sometimes bleeding open wounds. Scott and I were not bad kids at all; we were free labor to make M-80s and human punching bags for a couple of wacked-out parents!

One day, Jill and I had grabbed the oars and rowed a small boat across Spring Lake. Her mom came and picked her up at our house, so that meant I had to row it back. A few days later, I decided to do so. I called Jill, and she told me she would meet me at the inlet. Riding my Schwinn, I heard a loud crack; it came from the dark sky. I saw a friend who I went to school with; she was standing under her carport. I pulled in and started talking to her, as I pondered whether to go or not on that aluminum boat, then it started to rain. I was happy to be under that carport. Well, when the rain stopped, I'd go out and row that boat back. It rained for quite a while, so I finally decided to go home. Mom met me at the door, which was never a good sign. Screaming that Jill had called the Coast Guard and everyone was looking for me, then she started calling me a little bitch and a whore. She made two fists and beat the hell out of me.

When I was fifteen years old, mom and Walt decided that we were going to Disney World. Wow, this was the best thing ever! Well, at least I thought anyhow. We drove there; Disney World was awesome! Going there and back, I was car sick. I was always car sick, throwing up all over, and the headaches were awful. When I would vomit, the car would be pulled over, usually at a gas station. Mom would hand me a bucket and sponge and then tell me to clean it up. Sometimes I would keep throwing up; it was torture, literally. She could have given me motion-sickness pills, but no, I really believe that she did that to me on purpose.

On the way home, we stopped at a hotel. Mother told my brother and me we were going to sleep in the same bed. She looked at me with a warning that I was not to make a sound. Well, Scott was brutally pinching and kicking me, but I couldn't say anything. Being completely quiet, a tear silently came down my face. Oh God, help me. Mom saw it. She was outraged! Pulling me by my hair to the wall, she clutched onto my hair and ears. Slamming my head against the wall, back and forth, again and again. She was calling me every name in the book; I couldn't get away!

"Tammy, stop, you're going to kill her!" Walt pulled her off, the first and last time he ever stuck up for me. He probably remembered how he enjoyed jail last time he was in and did not want to go back in. I went to bed, crying myself to sleep, with a terrible headache, my hair pulled out, and a very heavy heart.

Chapter 5

YOU ARE NOBODY!

When I was fifteen years old, I finally found out I had a real father; his name was Jim. I was told by other friends that I was lucky because if Walt had never adopted me, he could never legally spank me. I asked my grandma if he had ever adopted me, and she said no. All of a sudden, I had some leverage. Finally, I had waited miserably all my life for this. The night before, Walt had kicked my bedroom door in because my mom and I had gotten into an argument. So I locked myself in my room. As soon as the door flew off the hinges, I knew I was in trouble. He beat me. As I rolled into a fetal position, he beat me so violently, I couldn't hold my battered body into a ball any longer. The only thing I could do was cry as the blows kept coming. But now, for the first time in my life, I had some leverage on that son of a bitch!

The next night, Walt was taking his frustrations out on my brother. I heard the cracking of the belt and my brother screaming. I stormed into his room and shouted, "Don't you ever touch my brother or me again, or I will call the police on you!" He stopped and didn't raise another hand that night. After school the next day, mom and Walt handed me some papers and explained how they were filing them the next day because I was an uncontrollable teenager. The papers were for a juvenile detention center. These two truly evil individuals had always had their way, and now I would have mine.

There was no shortage of cruelty between them; it never stopped. I replied that I was not going to the juvenile detention center; I was going to live with my real father, which scared me because I really didn't even know him. The fire was growing in my mother as she started her rampage. "Well, you little f——ing bitch, you go live with your worthless f——ing father, and I'll help you pack." She called my dad but didn't help me pack. I took a suitcase and my quilt, which my grandma had handmade for me out of dresses and skirts she had made for me throughout my childhood. I was almost to my dad's truck when my mom, the screaming banshee, ran behind me. "You will not take that quilt, it was made for your bed, and since you are not taking the bed, that stays here." Fine! I got about three feet from her and threw my quilt in her arms.

She slapped me in the face and called me an ungrateful bitch. Getting into the truck, my dad said, "It's okay, Dobbers (that's the nickname my dad gave me)."

My five-year-old sister Jenny just stared at me as the tears rolled down my beet-red cheek. In a very soft voice, she said to me, "It will be okay," as she looked directly into my eyes. I remember asking my mother if Jenny and Jamie were my real sisters since we had the same dad. I was really excited to think I could actually have sisters! She told me no because you have to have the same mother, not the same father. What a liar! My dad told me the truth: Yes, I did have two younger sisters, Jenny, five years old, and Jamie, seven years old. I felt so bad about leaving my brother behind, but now, with the little bit of leverage I had about the M-80s, there was a chance that I might say something to the authorities. I could only hope that Scott would stay safe. My stepmother didn't like me too well, but who could really blame her? She had just gotten a kid dumped on her from another marriage—another mouth to feed when they were barely making it. I tried to stay out of her way as much as possible.

After living with them for a year, I was told they were splitting up, and I would have to go back to my mom's. No, no, no. After actually living with a family that truly loved one another and loved me, the first time I ever felt love, unconditional love, I now had to go back to all the beatings and mental anguish again! So I ran away; of course, they tracked me down. I ran to Jill's house during a snowstorm. It was a long walk—around five miles. Dodging cars and dashing behind trees and bushes,

I finally came to my destination. Throwing snowballs at her bedroom window, I got her attention, with my finger to my lips for her to be quiet. Well, that went out the window as she started yelling, "Debbie's here! Debbie's here!" I was planning on spending the night in the garage, sharing it with the dog, but not anymore! Jill was crying as she gave me a big bear hug. She was so worried about me; nobody could find me, and cell phones were not invented yet. Her mom had to call my parents; she knew if she didn't, Tammy would go after her. My dad was laid off from work, but he said we would make it one way or another if I wanted to stay with him. Be a burden to my dad or live back with my psycho mom—not much of a choice. I had grown to love my dad, so I could not stand to be a burden to him.

At sixteen years old, I was working at A&W as a carhop, making $1.25 an hour plus tips. Then going to yet another school—yes, going back to live with my mom meant going to a different school again. This time, I actually didn't mind because it was the best school I had ever been to. Oh sure, I was scared, but the students and the teachers were genuinely caring and kind. Spring Lake High School was by far my favorite school. But there was still life at home.

Walt and his fireworks partner, Bill, had a warehouse full of fireworks in downtown Spring Lake. They had been there for over a year when Bill's son Tommy was extremely bored. He picked up a torch and started burning ants; the fire eventually found some powder and *kaboom*! The warehouse was exploding over and over again, box after box! It was a very large warehouse; it had a second floor with so many boxes of fireworks in it. There were public fireworks to put in his store, very large ones for the shows he would put on for the Coast Guard Festival and the Fourth of July, and, of course, his damn M-80s. We lived about four to five miles away from the warehouse. I heard a *boom*, *kaboom*, and thought, *Who is playing with fireworks out here?*

As I made it down the street, I looked across the lake and saw so much black smoke—it just filled the air. I was trying to think what was over there when Walt's car pulled into the driveway. He got out along with my mom and Cindy, his secretary. She had black soot all over her. She was so hysterical as she cried, I could hardly understand her. I had a sinking feeling that was the warehouse on fire, and yes, it was. Cindy said she barely made it out before the office was blown to smithereens. Wow, luckily nobody got killed, but Tommy had third-degree burns all over his body. He was in bad shape; he had many skin grafts, but he made it through and lived.

Making M-80 fireworks and the beatings started up again. We weren't allowed most of the time to have friends over. We were told friends would only get you into trouble. My brother and I were made to stay home; we had to skip school many times to help make the M-80s. One day, my hands were so cramped from squeezing glue into all of the small tubes that my fingers just could not move anymore. Asking my stepdad if I could take a break, he barked that nobody gets a break until all the work is done! As he slithered into the next room to mix the powders and smoke—yes, I said smoke—he always smoked around the black powder! I ran upstairs to run hot water on my hands to help the cramps. As I turned around, there he was, a red bloodshot-eyed devil. He yelled, "Who do you think you are!"

I didn't know what to say, so very quietly I answered, "Debbie."

He backhanded me across the face and bellowed at me again, "Who do you think you are?"

I was crying, and I didn't know what to say, so I said, "I don't know." A violent, harder slap across my face followed.

"*You are nobody!* You will never be anybody, you will always be nobody, do you understand?"

Sobbing, I answered yes. Torn up inside, I walked back downstairs to my workstation. I was sixteen years old now, and I just could not stand the abuse any longer. That was it—either they would kill me with the beatings or by the M-80 fireworks blowing up the house.

After dinner, I was told to go downstairs to my work station. As I reached the stairs, I told mom I had to go for a walk. Being the kind of control freak she was, she replied, "If you walk out that door, don't ever come back".

Through my tears, I explained to her how I needed some fresh air and I would be back in ten minutes. She repeated herself, and I didn't come back. At the age of sixteen, I left home. I was on my own now. I had my boyfriend, Bob, pick me up and moved in with his parents. Bob and I decided to move to Denton, Texas. I put myself in twelfth grade right away, and through my vocational school, I got my first secretarial job for an aeronautical engineer. Thank goodness this would be the last school I would have to go to. I graduated early in January and on the honor roll, so I thought I did pretty well. Bob had a job at a gas station / fast-food joint.

We ended up getting married shortly after I graduated, then that's when things started. One night, he knew I got up to get a glass of milk. I was coming back to bed, and as he came out of the bathroom-*bam*! He punched me right in the nose and said, "Don't ever sneak up on me like that again."

I was crying and screaming how bad it hurt and he told me to stop being such a baby, that's what I get for sneaking around in the dark. The next day, I had two black and blue eyes and a very swollen nose. I knew it was broken, but Bob wouldn't let me go to the hospital.

After a few months, I started a new job at the county appraisal/tax office. That was quite the job. Well, I decided to meet Bob at his work before they closed at 11:00 p.m. The problem was I got there at 10:00 p.m. They were closing, and Bob was already gone. Yep, that's right—they closed at

10:00, not 11:00 p.m. like he had told me all along. One of the employees was more than happy to tell me how he was having an affair with a sixty-three-year-old woman. I was just sick!

When he got home, I was packing my bags. He was apologizing and begging me to stay. I finally agreed, but I told him we would have to move out of the city. An old friend of his from Michigan offered him a carpentry job in Midland/Odessa, so he took it. Moving into a small one-bedroom apartment, I raised parakeets and cockatiels. Working full-time, this was a very hot climate to try to get used to, and the sandstorms were awful! After a year and not a tree in sight, it was time to move to lush Austin, Texas.

Chapter 6

I'm Sorry!

We arrived in Austin and then went to our room. Yes, we would be sharing a house with two other couples until we could get on our feet. His boss, Brent, with his pregnant wife, Camy; and in the other room with their own bathroom, Biff with his wife, Melba, and three daughters. Camy was nice, but I could tell Melba, with her snotty little sneers toward me, would be a tough one to get along with. I was always kind to everyone, especially Melba; I always put in extra effort when it came to her. She always wanted everything her way, and if it wasn't, she threw a fit. She was just a big bully. Even though there were five in her family, she wanted all groceries to be split three ways. I finally said, "No, thank you, we will buy our own groceries and cook our own meals."

That really pissed her off, and she had it out for me after that. Well, about two weeks shortly afterward, she decided to visit the guys at work, and she knew I was there. I had brought Bob his lunch when she made her way into the building, carrying her two-year-old daughter. Meeting up with Bob, she started yelling at him about how she didn't like the way I did this or that. Well, I walked back to my car, tried to get in, and Bob demanded my keys. When I didn't give them to him, he punched me in the face, right smack in the nose, and it popped so loud! Running behind the building, I sat down, crying and holding my face.

"Are you alright?" Karl quietly asked, trying to be a friend but not wanting Bob to see him either. I told Karl that Bob had punched me in the face. He replied he knew; everyone had seen it happen and told him to come out and check on me. If I was okay, Karl had to get back inside. Bob came around the corner just then and gave me the keys, no apology. He just said that next time he told me to do something, I better do it. So then it really started, the abuse from Bob. Of course, he came home that night with a dozen roses and apologized up and down, saying he would never hurt me again. So young and naive, I believed him.

Karl, Dave, and Jeff, his coworkers, were looking for a house to rent. They asked if we would like to look with them, and we jumped at the chance. We found a four-bedroom house, with three baths, two living rooms, and a dining room. It was nice. I was so happy to be out of the other house and in the new one with everyone from Michigan. It was pretty cool, we all became friends, especially Karl. He became a good friend to me, talking to me about how he and the guys had my back. and when they would hear Bob throwing things, yelling, and hitting the walls, they were there. Right outside my bedroom, ready to protect me if they heard me scream, but I would just cower and take it. Bob felt the protection for me; needless to say, we only lived there for two months. I was so homesick for Michigan and all of my friends there. I called mom to secure a place to stay.

It was a long ride on the Amtrak train, from Texas to Illinois and then to Michigan. I was picked up at the train station, and I was really happy to see my brother. He was having a hard life at home.

"Deb, mom bitches about everything, you know how it was, well, it still is."

"Yes, I remember all too well." I asked him if he was still getting hit. Funny, he had grown so tall, they didn't dare any longer.

After visiting family and friends for one week, I decided to stay another week. Mom told me to pack and be on my way.

"No, I was determined to stay. I couldn't shake this awful feeling; I could not go just then. She said I wasn't staying there; she would lock me out. Well, what would the neighbors think when they saw me sleeping on the lawn? Oh, she didn't like that! I cleaned up after dinner, then joined the others in front of the television. The news was on; there was an awful train wreck, and yes, it was an Amtrak train. They called it the Texas Eagle. It stops in Austin from Chicago, Illinois. I quickly ran upstairs to grab my train ticket and checked it. That was my train; I was supposed to be on that train! There were people killed when it derailed; my heart sank. I was furious with my mother and started yelling at her.

"That was my train, do you realize I could have been killed." She and my stepdad did not say one word to me, but Scott sure did. Scott couldn't stop talking about it; he asked me how I knew not to be on that train. I had the worst feeling, call it intuition, or I really believe it was divine intervention.

Another week went by, and then I was on that train back to Texas. Bob had bought us a new manufactured home. We moved it into a park in the Hill Country in Austin, about one mile from Willie Nelson's home. There was a bar across the street, and the owners knew Willie; he came to play there many times for them. I was always hoping I would get to see him; I just loved him, but I never did. His boss moved into this trailer park first; after work, the guys would get out of work and have a beer at the bar before going home.

The first night he came home and just smacked me around a little. He was never a drinker, but every night, he stopped at the bar, where he would drink more, and the beatings would get worse. As the days went on, the guys would pick him up for work so he would leave the car at home but always took the keys with him so I would have no transportation. He wouldn't allow me to have a telephone and would never give me any money, so I was totally dependent upon him. Every night, the beatings escalated, and now he was forcefully throwing me into the walls. As the bruises and cuts would heal, I would think to myself, *Did I deserve this? What was I doing to make him so angry at me? I must be doing something wrong, or why did my mom and stepdad beat me? Why does Bob drink and beat me?* So I just accepted that I was a bad person, I deserved it, and that I would try to be better.

One day, after he left for work, I started walking. The nearest pay phone was two miles away, and I wanted to call my mom. I finally made it to the phone and made a collect call. She answered, accepting the collect charges.

"Mom, please send me some money, I have to come home."

Mom said that I had to stay in Texas and work on my marriage.

"But mom," I replied, "Bob is beating me, and I can't take it anymore. He has already broken my nose two times."

"You probably deserved it." *Click.* The line went dead.

Wow, was I such a worthless human being? My own mother wouldn't help me? So off I went, back to the beatings again. Eventually, I had an idea: if he couldn't find me, he couldn't hit me. That night, I hid in the closet. My heart was pounding so loudly that it was thunderous in my ears, and I was so scared! He was yelling my name, ranting and raving about how sorry I was going to be when he got his hands on me. All of a sudden, silence. Ever so quietly, I slowly opened the door, and there he was—passed out on the bed. I ever so gently slipped into bed, not wanting to awaken the beast. He never remembered anything in the morning, so every night in the closet I went until he passed out.

One night he opened the closet, and I had put a blanket over myself and sat way in the back, in the corner. He was getting so close, and then he found me. Pulling me out, the painful beatings started up again.

At last, the day finally came that I didn't care any longer if I *lived or died*! So I decided to ask him for a divorce. He was actually surprised. But the beatings kept coming, and so did the apologies. "Oh I'm so sorry. I'll never do it again." Then flowers, candy, and small gifts. Then one night, he laid right on top of me.

I said, "Bob, get off me. I can't breathe." He said he wasn't going to let me leave. After two hours, he finally fell asleep, and I pushed him off. I had to stand and breathe deeply; I honestly thought I would have suffocated. The next day, he said he wanted to take me somewhere. I asked where, and he replied that it was a surprise. It was almost dark, and I couldn't imagine where he was taking me.

All of a sudden, he said, "Isn't Lake Dallas beautiful?" We were almost there when he yelled, "If I can't have you, nobody will!" He floored it, and right before we went over the dam, he turned the car sideways and came to a screeching stop. The wheels on my side went up and then slammed down. I was livid! I flung open the door and stood up; my rubbery legs were just shaking. I told him to leave me the hell alone. He squealed out of there, and I ran across the street to the beach, yes, pay phones.

I called my best friend Jill in Michigan, but she wasn't home; her dad was, and he wanted to know what was wrong. I always called him dad; he would give me big bear hugs, tell me I was a good kid, and say, "Love ya." He could tell I was really shaken up, so I proceeded to tell him. He talked to me for about thirty minutes until I could calm down some. As I told him that I loved him, he said the same back, then the cold click of the phone—I was alone again. Dreading the five-mile walk home in the dark, I got started on it, and guess who pulled up next to me? Bob. He was demanding I get in the car.

"Never again will I get in the car with you," I said. I finished my walk home on my own two feet. The next day, here come the apologies and the flowers. I told him I was going back home to Michigan. He asked how I was getting there because I wasn't taking the car.

I don't need the car. I'm hitchhiking. One way or another, I am going back home. If I stayed here, I would die. He would kill me. Even if I hitchhiked, at least I would have a chance of getting back home. Here, I have none. I don't need my mother's money or his stinking car.

The sun was rising, and I went to my friend Bev's home. She was from Spring Lake, Michigan, and had a five-week-old baby girl. I told her I was hitching my way back home. She said that in just a couple of days, they were driving back and that I could go with them if I'd like.

Oh yes, I was thrilled. Her father was a minister in Spring Lake, Michigan. More divine intervention, I think so!"

The day came, and Bob stated he was coming along—the girls in one car, the boys in another. Fine with me because I wasn't getting in a car with him! Bev had put her baby in a cardboard box, placing her in the back seat. I felt that wasn't right but didn't know; I had never had a baby. We drove nonstop, except for gas. We were supposed to trade off drivers. Didn't realize Bev was such a bad driver, and after only an hour of her driving, I just could not take it any longer. I had to take the wheel back. As Bev drove, she kept slamming on the brakes, which kept slamming me into the dash. I drove all the way back to Michigan, making my arrival. I was totally exhausted.

Chapter 7

BE STRONG!

My friend Kathi's dad owned a video store in 1983, when VCRs were just invented and you could rent one, or if you had one, you could watch movies in your own home. Kathi and I moved into an apartment right above the video store. But Bob would not leave me alone. He relentlessly called and pounded on my door. I felt I would go crazy until my boss, Jake, brought me down to the police station and showed me how to file a restraining order against him. Kathi told me about a center for women who have been abused. Well, that could not have been for me; I wasn't abused. I deserved everything I got, my mom told me so. She finally talked me into it. "What? Would it hurt?" she said. I decided to go; what could it hurt?

I introduced myself to the counselor, and for the full hour, all I did was cry, and she handed me tissue after tissue. She was so kind, and the next week, I went again. She asked me about my childhood. I told her I came because of being abused by my soon-to-be ex-husband. Besides, my childhood really had nothing to do with it. She started asking me questions, and I found out it had a lot to do with why I felt so worthless. Bob, of course, was stalking me. As soon as I left, he went in and demanded to know what I told them. She asked him if he would like a police escort off the premises; he left.

Then he went to pick up his mother and proceeded to bring her to my apartment. "Why are you leaving my son? He's such a good boy, can't you work on things with him?" That was it; he had gone too far dragging in his poor mother who thought him a saint.

I looked at him and said, "Okay, you have brought this on yourself!" I told her how he had gotten into porn, cheated on me with a sixty-three-year-old woman, became a total alcoholic, and continued to beat on me over and over again, even breaking my nose twice. She grabbed him by the ear and pulled him all the way out to the car. All I could hear were screams of, "Mom, stop! Mom!"

Returning to Women In Transition (WIT), the counselor unraveled my life little by little, week by week. I actually learned that all of this was not my fault. I couldn't believe it; I was not a bad person! I had never known anything else. I went from one abusive home to another. I grew up with it and then married into it. *It is never okay for anyone to hit you!*

Later in life, I figured out that my mother was quite narcissistic and very mentally ill, as was my grandmother and great-grandmother. I asked God to give me the strength to forgive her, but these scars were deep, and I could never forget. My best friend Jill would always ask me how I could still love her. After all she has done to me and my brother, she is still my mom, so I push the bad things aside and always keep my guard up. God says to honor thy father and thy mother, so I asked for His strength to do so. They finally got busted by the ATF; the feds finally caught them.

They were renting a building right by Grand Haven High School, across from their football field. They risked the lives of many people; there was so much black powder and finished M-80s in that building.

As far as Bob goes, he found another girlfriend and married right after our divorce. Me, well, session after session, for over a year, I learned that it was okay to love again, and I did. Now Ed and I started dating, and things were going well. He drank a little beer, smoked a little marijuana, and had a little bit of a bad habit. Come to find out, he liked a little white line, which became a very big deal, especially when he was trying to get me to do it. We were together for three years, and in the beginning, things were good, as with all relationships. But as time went on, the mental abuse reared its ugly head and started up. Little comments like, "How can you manage a video store and be so stupid!" Then he tried to alienate me from my friends, telling me that everyone knows I was a lesbian with my best friends Jill and Kathi. Then came the cocaine. He would say, "If you just try it one time, you'll really like it."

I didn't want to try it; I didn't want to get hooked on it and didn't want to give it a chance to destroy my life. He wanted me to marry him. I told him not with the way things were. He promised he would quit using cocaine if I married him. I accepted; I was a fool. We were married for one month, then I left him. He never tried to quit; he just used more and more. I ended up going back for a while. It is so amazing to me that the person who is supposed to love you can belittle you so much that you actually believe you are worthless. Once you are in that grip, it is so difficult to break free and realize that you are worth something and yes, you really do matter!

After bringing me to his sister's one night, he brought me upstairs, and there were so many people, you could barely push your way down the hall. We made it to the bedroom, and he said, "Over here on the dresser, they're all lined up for you." I looked, and there were a bunch of white lines on mirrors on the dresser. The pressure was building, and I was feeling it. Ed said, "Hurry up and snort a line, everyone is watching you."

I whispered to him, "No."

He said that I better do it, or everybody is going to think I was a nark. That was it; I stormed out of that room. I didn't give a rat's ass what anyone thought; I went into the living room. Ed came down, and I told him to take me home or I was walking. So he did. I thought that was too easy, and as soon as we got in the house, he said, "I brought some home because I thought you might have been too shy to do it in front of everyone."

He never did break me, and I did leave right after that. I did go back to Women in Transition. They were great. They helped me get my self-esteem back and made me feel like I mattered once again.

I thought that would be it for me. I had two chances at love; neither had worked out. So I definitely was not looking; I just wanted to be left alone. My friend Sherry, who worked with me at the video store, was getting married in a couple of months. One of her bridesmaids was pregnant and figured she would be quite large by the time Sherry had her wedding, so she asked me if I would step in as a bridesmaid. I said sure; it sounded like it would be fun, and it was! She had me walk down the aisle with her brother, Phill.

One year later, we were married. Now we have three beautiful daughters, Amber Lyn, Heather Renae, and Rachel

Ann. So we have been married for thirty-six years now and just became proud grandparents. Mikey is fabulous!

When you feel like there is no hope, there is always hope, but you must be willing to leave the bad situation. Unfortunately, a lot of women stay with an abusive partner because they love them and believe they will change. Do not fool yourself, or you may be another statistic in the graveyard. Get away, get help, and live your life the way you should. Most abuse centers will give you free counseling if you have no money. Also, they will hide you and your children. They will place you in safe houses, which they have everywhere. Please don't be a victim any longer; you can do it. You can live life free of hitting, physical, and mental abuse. You are worth it; you are not worthless! Be brave, take your life back before you don't have a choice and it's taken from you.